CORNE[RSTONES]
OF FRE[EDOM]

D0451913

U.S. INFRASTRUCTURE
BY DEBORAH KENT

CHILDREN'S PRESS®
An Imprint of Scholastic Inc.
New York   Toronto   London   Auckland   Sydney
Mexico City   New Delhi   Hong Kong
Danbury, Connecticut

BRINGING HISTORY to LIFE

Content Consultant
James Marten, PhD
Professor and Chair, History Department
Marquette University
Milwaukee, Wisconsin

Library of Congress Cataloging-in-Publication Data
Kent, Deborah.
 U.S. infrastructure / by Deborah Kent.
 pages cm.—(Cornerstones of freedom)
 Includes bibliographical references and index.
 Audience: Ages 9–12.
 Audience: Grades 4 to 6
 ISBN 978-0-531-28208-3 (lib. bdg.) — ISBN 978-0-531-27673-0 (pbk.)
 1. Infrastructure (Economics)—United States. 2. Public utilities—United
States. 3. Electricity—United States. 4. Transportation—United States. I.
Title. II. Title: US infrastructure.
 HC110.C3K455 2014
 388.0973—dc23   2013002135

1 2 3 4 5 6 7 8 9 10 R 23 22 21 20 19 18 17 16 15 14

Photographs © 2014: age footstock/Everett Collection: 5 top, 23, 57 top;
Alamy Images: 36 (Pictorial Press Ltd.), 21 (World History Archive); AP
Images: 50 (Bebeto Matthews), 44 (Manuel Balce Ceneta), 4 top, 8, 10,
11, 14, 27, 30 (North Wind Picture Archives), 5 bottom, 33; Corbis Images/
Bettmann: 32; Dreamstime/Georgios: 37; Getty Images: 18; Hoover Dam
Bypass/FHWA/CFLHD: cover; iStockphoto/Xavier Arnau: 46; Library of
Congress: 4, 15, 17, 22, 26, 28, 29, 34, 39, 56, 57 bottom; Newscom/akg-
images: 25; Shutterstock, Inc.: 7 (Christian Delbert), 6 (Lucarelli Temistocle);
Superstock, Inc.: back cover (Caren Brinkema/Science Faction), 40, 47,
48 (ClassicStock.com); The Granger Collection: 13; The Image Works:
51 (Marjorie Kamys Cotera/Daemmrich Photos), 38 (Mary Evans Picture
Library), 43 (Mary Evans/Pharcide), 54 (Melanie Stetson Freeman/Christian
Science Monitor), 55 (Peter Hvizdak), 2, 3, 20 (SZ Photo/Scherl), 16 (ullstein
bild); Thinkstock/iStockphoto: 42, 45; XNR Productions, Inc.: 52, 53.

Did you know that studying history can be fun?

BRING HISTORY TO LIFE by becoming a history investigator. Examine the evidence (primary and secondary source materials); cross-examine the people and witnesses. Take a look at what was happening at the time—but be careful! What happened years ago might suddenly become incredibly interesting and change the way you think!

Contents

SETTING THE SCENE
A Hidden Network.........6

CHAPTER 1
Big Plans for a New Nation 8

CHAPTER 2
Riding the Rails 18

CHAPTER 3
The Power of Electricity 30

CHAPTER 4
Connections and Concerns 40

MAP OF THE EVENTS

What Happened Where?................ 52

THE STORY CONTINUES

Today and Tomorrow ... 54

Influential Individuals 56
Timeline 58
Living History 60
Resources 6 1
Glossary 62
Index 63
About the Author..............64

A Hidden Network

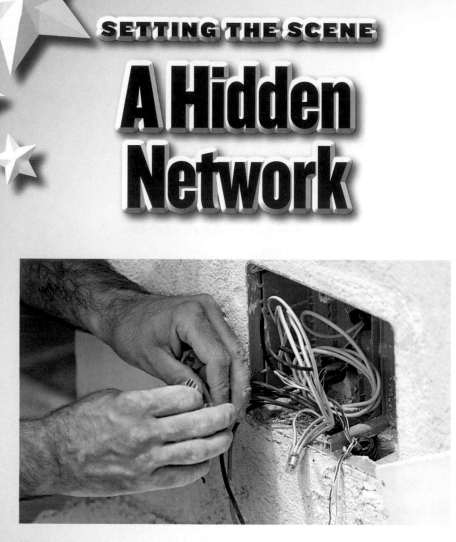

The switches and outlets on your walls are connected to a network of wires that move electricity around your house.

Your house is full of secrets. A web of cables and wires is tucked out of sight inside the walls. A network of pipes lies hidden beneath the floors. The wires and cables bring electricity, telephone service, and the Internet into your home. The pipes bring in clean water for drinking and bathing. They carry dirty water away when you wash the dishes or flush the toilet.

The network of pipes and cables in your home is a tiny part of the country's vast **infrastructure**. The infrastructure is made up of many systems that work together. The transportation system includes roads and highways, railroad tracks, bridges, and tunnels. Telephone wires and cell phone towers belong to the telecommunications system. Other systems within the infrastructure provide power, water, and **sanitation**.

The U.S. infrastructure developed gradually throughout the country's history, and its growth has often been a controversial political issue. To understand today's infrastructure, we must learn how it grew and changed over the centuries.

Cellular towers and other antennas send communication signals through the air.

CHAPTER 1

BIG PLANS
FOR A NEW NATION

American colonists built
their own homes using
wood cut from nearby trees.

IN 1607, COLONISTS established the first permanent North American English settlement at Jamestown, Virginia. In the decades that followed, 13 English colonies sprang up along the Atlantic coast from Georgia to New Hampshire.

During the colonial era, people heated their homes with wood-burning fireplaces. The dense forests provided all the firewood the colonists needed. Farmers raised most of their own food. Horse-drawn wagons brought fruits, vegetables, and meat from farms to markets in nearby towns. Riders on horseback carried messages and letters from town to town or from one colony to another. Most people never moved far from their birthplaces. They didn't have much need to visit or communicate with people far away.

For American settlers, the journey west on unpaved trails was long and hard. It took settlers up to six months to reach their new homes.

Westward Ho!

In 1776, the American colonies broke away from Great Britain. The 13 former colonies became one nation, the United States of America. A vast stretch of untamed land sprawled to the west. Americans were eager to farm the land west of the Allegheny Mountains. The U.S. government encouraged their dreams, and the nation expanded as people moved westward.

The settlers moved on foot, on horseback, in wagons, or by boat. They often followed trails that had been made long ago by Native Americans. There were few roads as we know them today.

The federal government funded a major road-building project to help the settlers travel more easily. Construction of the National Road began in 1811 at

Cumberland, Maryland. The road crossed the Allegheny Mountains and pushed through the forests to Wheeling, West Virginia. By 1838, it reached all the way to the village of Vandalia, Illinois. Altogether, the National Road stretched 620 miles (998 kilometers).

Travel along the National Road was no easy task. The road was unpaved. Rainstorms turned it into a river of mud. To ease travel, crews placed split logs flat side up along the muddiest sections. These reinforced portions

The National Road was also known as the Cumberland Road.

were called corduroy roads because the rough planks reminded travelers of the ridges on corduroy fabric.

No one used the word *infrastructure* when the National Road was being built. Yet the construction of the National Road was an early step toward creating the infrastructure of the United States.

Rivers served as natural highways for the westbound travelers. Pioneers pushed westward on log rafts and hastily constructed flatboats. Boats loaded with neighing horses, barking dogs, and mooing cows floated in noisy caravans. However, rivers do not always run where people want to go.

Leaders in the state of New York longed for a water route that would connect the Hudson River with the Great Lakes. In 1817, New Yorkers raised $7 million to build the Erie Canal. Some 9,000 laborers spent eight years digging a trench that measured 363 miles (584 km) in length. The canal connected the Hudson River port of Albany with the city of Buffalo on Lake Erie. When the Erie Canal opened in 1825, boats could carry goods up the Hudson from New York City all the way to the Great Lakes.

A FIRSTHAND LOOK AT
THE ERIE CANAL MUSEUM

The Erie Canal Museum is located in Syracuse, New York. The museum is housed in the Weighlock Building, which dates back to 1850. At one time, canal boats were built and repaired in this building. See page 60 for a link to learn more about the museum.

Many of those who helped build the Erie Canal went on to help build other canals in the United States.

The Erie Canal brought boom times to the state of New York. Cities along the canal, such as Buffalo and Syracuse, prospered with the increase in trade. New York City, at the mouth of the Hudson, gained most of all. Coal from Pennsylvania and wheat from Ohio flowed through the canal and into the big city.

The success of the Erie Canal inspired other states to build canals of their own. The U.S. government recognized that canals benefited the nation as a whole, and it helped fund many canal-building projects. By 1840, some 3,000 miles (4,828 km) of canals zigzagged across portions of Delaware, Virginia, New Jersey, Ohio, and Illinois.

The Erie Canal was 40 feet (12 meters) wide and 4 feet (1.2 m) deep.

Along the sides of the canals ran narrow roads called **towpaths**. Mules trudged along the towpaths, tugging loaded canal boats that floated on the muddy water. In towns along the way, markets sold goods to passengers and mule drivers. Factories built new canal boats and repaired old ones. But the booming canal era did not last for long.

The Power of Steam

In 1698, a British inventor named Thomas Savery built a machine for pumping water out of coal mines. The machine was powered by steam that was produced by burning wood or coal. Steam-driven engines were used in the mining **industry** throughout the 18th century. Steam also powered machines used in the production of textiles.

John Fitch, an American inventor and businessman, realized that steam could be used to power boats. In 1788, he started a steamboat service on the Delaware River between Philadelphia, Pennsylvania, and Burlington, New Jersey. The service drew interest, but it never made much money.

The world's first commercially successful steamboat was built by American **engineer** Robert Fulton. In 1807, Fulton built a steam powered paddle wheel ship called the *Clermont*. The *Clermont* carried passengers up the Hudson River from New York City to Albany. On its first run, it made the 150-mile (241 km) journey in 32 hours. Its average speed of 5 miles per hour (8 kph) seems slow today, but it was amazingly fast to people who were used to rowing or paddling.

Three years later, Fulton constructed an

Robert Fulton

As a child, Robert Fulton (1765–1815) loved to tinker with mechanical devices. Fulton trained as an artist, but he soon shifted to engineering. In addition to building the first widely used steamboat, he made several other major contributions to water travel. In the early 19th century, he worked with the British government to develop one of the world's first submarines. He also helped develop a system of canals in England.

even larger steamboat called the *New Orleans*. It carried passengers and freight down the Ohio and Mississippi Rivers. The steamboat made the journey from Pittsburgh, Pennsylvania, to New Orleans, Louisiana. However, it was not powerful enough to complete the return trip against the river's mighty current.

By 1830, many steam-powered vessels traveled the Mississippi and Missouri Rivers. One major shipbuilder was Henry Shreve. Shreve designed vessels especially for the shallow waters of the Mississippi. His boats sat high on the water. Their engines were on the main deck instead of being carried below. The city of Shreveport, Louisiana, is named in Shreve's honor.

Most steamboats were poorly built and lasted only four or five years before falling into disrepair.

River steamboats acquired a certain elegance as more and more were built. Some people called them "wedding cakes" because their decks were often covered with fancy decorations. The wail of a steamboat whistle could carry more than a mile. When they heard the shrill whistle, villagers rushed to the wharves to find out what new people or exotic freight had arrived. Steamboats carried everything from bales of cotton and barrels of molasses to pianos. Steamboats moved people and goods faster than ever before. Yet they had serious limitations. Steamboats could travel only on large rivers. Soon, a new form of travel would help solve this problem.

SPOTLIGHT ON

Mark Twain

The American writer Samuel Clemens used the pen name Mark Twain. He is best known for his novels *The Adventures of Tom Sawyer* and *The Adventures of Huckleberry Finn*. Clemens chose his pen name while he worked on Mississippi River steamboats as a young man. It came from a phrase used by the crew. To measure the depth of the river, a crew member held a rope with a weight on the end. When the weight scraped the bottom, the crewman knew how deep the water was. If the depth was 2 fathoms (12 feet, or 3.7 meters), the crewman shouted, "Mark twain!" *Twain* is an old word meaning "two."

CHAPTER 2

RIDING THE RAILS

The Baltimore and Ohio Railroad opened in 1830 and remains a freight route today.

ON JULY 4, 1828, A CROWD gathered in Baltimore, Maryland. As spectators cheered, an old man dug a spade into the earth. The man with the spade was Charles Carroll of Maryland, the last surviving signer of the Declaration of Independence. He was breaking ground for the construction of the Baltimore and Ohio Railroad. "I consider what I have just now done to be among the most important acts of my life, second only to my signing the Declaration of Independence," Carroll stated.

Horse-drawn railcars were used to transport logs and other resources out of the wilderness.

Travel on the Tracks

Early in the 19th century, people in the United States started using horses and mules to pull wagons along tracks. The tracks were made of wood and protected by a layer of iron. They allowed the wagons to travel quickly and smoothly. These early track systems were known as railroads.

The Granite Railway was completed in 1826. It is considered the first commercial railroad in the United States. "Trains" of three horse-drawn wagons hauled stone along the railroad to Boston Harbor from a quarry in Quincy, Massachusetts. By 1830, two similar lines were carrying coal from mines in northeastern Pennsylvania.

Horse-drawn rail wagons were a vast improvement over wagons that ran on dirt roads. The rails kept wagons from sinking in the mud or snagging on rocks and logs. However, horse-drawn vehicles were slow, and they could haul only a limited amount of weight. Engineers looked for a better system—one that would use steam power to pull cars along railroad tracks.

American engineers who visited Great Britain were impressed by the railroads they saw. The British railroads used giant steam-powered engines called **locomotives**. In 1829, an American engineer named Horatio Allen purchased an 8-ton British-built locomotive called the *Stourbridge Lion*. The locomotive was so huge it had to be taken apart for the voyage across the Atlantic Ocean. It was carefully reassembled when it arrived in the United States.

Before getting involved with the railroad business, Horatio Allen worked on the Chesapeake and Delaware Canal and the Delaware and Hudson Canal.

Crowds watched in amazement as Allen drove the *Stourbridge Lion* along a track that included a bridge high above a river. The bridge groaned and shook under the locomotive's tremendous weight. Allen did not complete the 6-mile (10 km) run. Because of this failure, the engine never was used again.

In 1830, a horse-drawn train raced against an American-built locomotive called the *Tom Thumb*. The *Tom Thumb* was built by Peter Cooper of New York. It held the lead for most of the race. However, the locomotive broke down as it approached the finish line. The *Tom Thumb* ground to a stop while the horse pulled its car to victory.

After its failure, the *Stourbridge Lion* was placed into storage until 1849, when it was disassembled and used for parts.

In addition to building the _Tom Thumb_ locomotive, Peter Cooper ran for president in 1876.

The fates of the _Stourbridge Lion_ and the _Tom Thumb_ did not reduce enthusiasm for railroad development. Instead, these failures taught inventors important lessons and helped them build better railroads. By 1835, the United States had more than 1,000 miles (1,609 km) of railroad track. Around 200 railroad companies held operating licenses. As they carried more and more passengers and freight, railroads became an essential part of the nation's infrastructure.

A VIEW FROM ABROAD

In 1842, the English writer Charles Dickens toured the United States. In his book *American Notes*, he described his ride on a train in Massachusetts. "There is a great deal of jolting, a great deal of noise, a great deal of wall, not much window, a locomotive engine, a shriek, and a bell," he wrote. Dickens noted that in the United States, rich people and poor people rode together in the same car. English trains had first-, second-, and third-class carriages. Third-class tickets were the cheapest ones. First-class tickets cost more, but offered more space and comfort to passengers.

The Iron Horse

Trains changed the way people lived in the United States. Before railroads became common, the average American seldom traveled more than a few miles from home. Then came the thundering steam engine, puffing smoke and sounding its whistle. The Iron Horse, as it came to be called by some, whisked people from one far-flung town to another at speeds of 20 to 30 miles per hour (32 to 48 kph). The novelist Nathaniel Hawthorne wrote, "Railroads are positively the greatest blessing that the ages have wrought out for us. They give us wings."

Train travel was fast, but no one claimed it was comfortable. Passengers coughed from the smoke and avoided flying cinders.

The U.S. government encouraged the development of railroads during the late 19th century. Railroad companies were given free land and federal funds to help them expand. Towns competed to lure the railroad companies. Towns that got railroad stations flourished. All too often, towns without stations withered away.

No city benefited from railroads more than Chicago. In 1800, Chicago was a cluster of settlers' cabins on the swampy shore of Lake Michigan. By 1890, its population topped one million, making it the second-largest city in the United States. Never before had a city grown at such an explosive rate. Chicago achieved this incredible

Cotton was among the many goods shipped in and out of Chicago's train stations in the late 19th century.

The United States acquired more than 500,000 square miles (1,300,000 sq km) of land in the Mexican-American War.

growth largely because it was a central hub for railroads heading north, south, east, and west. Railroads had become a vital part of the nation's infrastructure.

Manifest Destiny

Throughout the 19th century, American settlers continued to travel westward. Many Americans believed that the nation was destined to stretch from the Atlantic coast to the shores of the Pacific Ocean. The United States purchased the vast Louisiana Territory from France in 1803. It also captured much of New Mexico, Arizona, and California in the Mexican-American War from 1846 to 1848. By 1848, the nation reached from ocean to ocean.

In 1848, a ranch foreman found a pebble of gold in a California streambed. News of the discovery drew huge numbers of gold seekers to California, and new towns sprouted up quickly. California's population zoomed from 15,000 in 1847 to 92,000 in 1850.

Far from their friends and families back east, many of the newcomers felt lonely. A trip from the East Coast to the West Coast by stagecoach or wagon might take months. It might take a letter several months to reach a settlement in the goldfields. The United States faced an infrastructure crisis. Only the railroads could bind the huge country together.

Around two billion dollars' worth of gold was mined during the California gold rush.

The Civil War

The Civil War (1861–1865) erupted when 11 Southern states attempted to break away from the United States. The North overwhelmed the South largely because it had a more industrial **economy** and more advanced infrastructure. Trains played a critical role in the war by carrying soldiers, food, and military supplies across the Northern states. The North had some 25,000 miles (40,234 km) of railroad tracks, compared to only 10,000 miles (16,093 km) of tracks in the South.

In 1854, railroad tracks reached as far west as the Mississippi River at Rock Island, Illinois. A passenger could board a train in New York City and arrive in Illinois only two days later. Engineers planned the next step in railroad construction. They were determined to lay tracks all the way to California.

In 1866, two companies began to build tracks that would help complete the link from east to west. The Union Pacific began laying tracks westward from Omaha, Nebraska. The Central Pacific started its work in Sacramento, California, and extended tracks toward the east. At first, it was uncertain where the two construction crews would meet.

For three years, the two companies worked feverishly to build the great rail line. They built bridges over rivers and carved tunnels through mountains. The

The transcontinental railroad spanned almost 1,800 miles (3,000 km) of track.

construction effort developed into a race to see which crew could lay the most track.

In the spring of 1869, the two construction crews finally met at Promontory Summit, Utah. In a grand ceremony, a golden spike was driven into the rails to mark the completion of the first **transcontinental** railroad. Two engines faced each other and edged forward until they gently touched.

A FIRSTHAND LOOK AT
THE NATIONAL RAILROAD MUSEUM

Since 1958, the National Railroad Museum in Green Bay, Wisconsin, has been showing visitors how railroads shaped the United States. Visitors can view more than 70 railcars and locomotive engines. See page 60 for a link to view more information about the museum.

CHAPTER 3
THE POWER OF ELECTRICITY

As electricity and communication lines began to spread across the country, sending messages over long distances became much easier.

THROUGHOUT MOST OF HUMAN history, communication across long distances was slow and unreliable. Runners or riders on horseback carried news from town to town. A letter from overseas might take six months to reach its destination, if it ever got there at all.

Scientific discoveries in the 18th and 19th centuries set the stage for a breakthrough in communication. When scientists learned to harness the power of electricity, new communication systems became possible. These systems soon formed crucial parts of the nation's infrastructure.

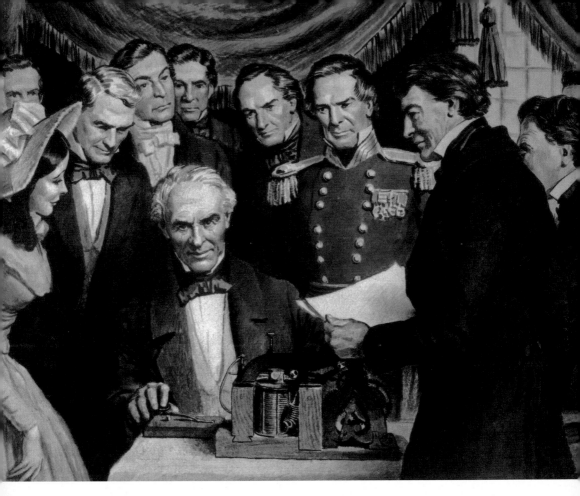

Before inventing the telegraph, Samuel F. B. Morse (seated) had become a skilled painter.

The Lightning Line

On May 24, 1844, an inventor named Samuel F. B. Morse sat in the chamber of the U.S. Supreme Court in Washington, D.C. Using a new machine he had invented, he tapped out a coded message. The message flashed along a wire that stretched to a similar machine 40 miles (64 km) away in Baltimore, Maryland. In Baltimore, Morse's assistant, Alfred Vail, read the historic words: "What hath God wrought?" Morse had sent the world's first telegraph message.

Samuel Morse was not the first person to experiment with sending messages by using electricity. Sixty-one people in the United States and Europe claimed to have invented the telegraph. However, Morse was the first inventor to make the telegraph a commercial success. He persuaded Congress to fund a telegraph line from Washington, D.C., to New York. Soon several telegraph companies operated in other parts of the country as well. The telegraph was sometimes called the lightning line, and telegraph operators were called lightning slingers.

In 1858, workers achieved an astonishing feat of engineering. They laid an underwater cable all the way across the Atlantic Ocean. U.S. president James Buchanan

YESTERDAY'S HEADLINES

During the 1844 Democratic National Convention in Baltimore, Maryland, Samuel Morse's telegraph dazzled the public by sending up-to-the-minute news of the convention to Washington, D.C. A reporter for the *New York Herald* wrote, "Little else is done here but watch Professor Morse's bulletin from Baltimore, to learn the progress of doings at Convention."

On October 24, 1861, a telegram was sent from San Francisco, California, to President Abraham Lincoln in Washington, D.C., to let him know that the transcontinental telegraph line was operational.

and Great Britain's queen Victoria exchanged greetings across 3,000 miles (4,828 km) of rolling waves. The fastest-growing telegraph company was called Western Union. In 1861, Western Union completed the first transcontinental telegraph line.

Like the railroads, the telegraph helped bind the growing nation together. It became an essential element in the nation's infrastructure. However, another new invention soon pushed the telegraph into the background.

"Mister Watson, Come Here!"

During the 1870s, several inventors worked on devices that would use wires to transmit the human voice. The most successful was the telephone, invented by Alexander Graham Bell. On March 10, 1877, Bell spoke to his assistant, Thomas Watson, using the instrument he had invented. "Mister Watson," he said, "come here! I want to see you." It was the world's first telephone conversation.

A VIEW FROM ABROAD

When the transatlantic cable was complete, many people hoped it would herald an era of world peace. They believed that world leaders would be able to solve their differences through discussions instead of fighting wars. A reporter for the *Times of London* wrote, "Tomorrow the hearts of the civilized world will beat in a single pulse, and from that time forth forevermore the continental divisions of the earth will, in a measure, lose those conditions of time and distance which now mark their relations."

In the early years of the telephone, there were no central systems to direct calls between different people. If two friends wanted to use the new gadget, they had to directly connect a pair of phones, one in each house. They could use their phones only to call each other.

A FIRSTHAND LOOK AT
THE MUSEUM OF COMMUNICATIONS

The Museum of Communications in Seattle, Washington, traces the history of the telephone. Exhibits include antique telephones and switchboard equipment, a collection of photographs, and a model of Alexander Graham Bell's first working telephone. See page 60 for a link to learn more about the museum.

Soon telephone companies set up central switchboards that could handle many calls at once. By 1904, more than three million telephones were in service in the United States.

Telephone switchboard operators plugged and unplugged lines to connect different callers.

Alexander Melville Bell began going by the name Alexander Graham Bell at age 11, in tribute to a family friend named Alexander Graham.

In 1915, telephone lines spanned the country. From New York City, Alexander Graham Bell made the first coast-to-coast long-distance call. Once again, he spoke to Thomas Watson. However, this time Watson was in faraway San Francisco, California.

As telephone communication became more widespread, it became an essential part of personal life. Today's businesses and government offices could not function without it.

Natural gas is harvested from deep underground.

Wired!

After the Civil War, natural gas began to provide lighting and heat for people who lived in cities. The use of natural gas required important developments in the infrastructure. Gas entered homes and businesses through a network of underground pipes. Pipes also provided running water, and a system of sewers carried away wastewater.

By the late 1870s, electricity was used to light city streets. It was also used in certain hotels and restaurants. A young inventor named Thomas Edison was convinced that electricity could be used to provide inexpensive lighting in the home. At his laboratory in Menlo Park, New Jersey, Edison devised an incandescent electric lightbulb in 1879. An incandescent bulb contains a small piece of a metal called tungsten, which gives off light as it slowly burns. Edison's first lightbulb could last for 40 hours. In 1880, Edison developed a better lightbulb that could burn for 1,200 hours.

In 1883, Edison created the first centralized power system. It lit up the city of Brockton, Massachusetts. In the next few years, many more cities installed electric power stations.

SPOTLIGHT ON

Thomas Edison

When he attended school in Port Huron, Michigan, young Thomas Edison pestered his teacher with endless questions. The teacher decided that Edison suffered from a scrambled brain and could not be taught. Edison left school and was instead homeschooled by his parents. He soon began to learn with astonishing speed. Edison is credited with more than 1,000 inventions, including the first voting machine, the phonograph, and the motion picture.

CHAPTER 4

CONNECTIONS AND CONCERNS

By the 1930s, telephones were becoming common in homes and offices throughout the United States.

BY THE DAWN OF THE 20TH century, an extensive system of roads and railroads crisscrossed the nation. People throughout the country were linked by telegraph and telephone lines. A growing number of homes had electricity and running water. The infrastructure of the United States kept people in touch and provided the comforts of modern life. Since then, the infrastructure has been improved and expanded to meet the demands of new technology and a growing population.

People in the United States use over 400 billion gallons
(1.5 trillion liters) of water per day.

The Importance of Stability

Today, the U.S. infrastructure works so well that most
people do not even have to think about it. When you
flip a switch, you expect the lights to turn on. When you
twist a faucet, you assume that clean water will flow. You
count on cell phone and Internet service to keep you in
touch with the world.

U.S. society depends on an infrastructure that works
smoothly and flawlessly. Trouble can result when any part
of the infrastructure stops working. A breakdown in the
infrastructure can pose a threat to property and human life.

A Nation on the Move

There are more than 250 million trucks and cars in the United States today. These vehicles drive along 4 million miles (6.4 million km) of streets and highways. Taken together, these roadways would circle the planet 160 times!

The Lincoln Highway opened to traffic in 1913. It was the first highway to stretch across the country from coast to coast. A driver could travel 3,142 miles (5,057 km) across 14 states, straight from New York City to San Francisco, California, with hardly a turn or zigzag. The Lincoln Highway was hailed as a modern marvel.

Today, a system of interstate highways serves the entire United States. The highway system was created in the 1950s under the leadership of President Dwight D.

The Lyons-Fulton Bridge carried traffic on the Lincoln Highway across the Mississippi River.

A FIRSTHAND LOOK AT
THE LINCOLN HIGHWAY

The century-old Lincoln Highway is still in use today. In fact, loyal fans enjoy driving the road from end to end. The highway runs from Times Square in the heart of New York City to San Francisco's Lincoln Park. Along the way, the highway is marked by posts that display the giant letter *L*. See page 60 for a link to learn more about the highway online.

Eisenhower. As a young army officer in 1919, Eisenhower led military trucks from Washington, D.C., to San Francisco. The trucks followed the Lincoln Highway wherever they could, but they were sometimes forced to move over back roads. Most of the back roads between Illinois and California were unpaved. As a result, the cross-country trip took more than a week. Eisenhower

The U.S. road system spans around 4 million miles (6.4 million km).

NORT

INTERSTAT

270

concluded that the country must build an efficient highway system to keep its economy and defense strong. The federal highway system was begun in 1957, when Eisenhower was serving as president. By 2010, the network of interstate highways extended more than 47,182 miles (75,932 km).

Serious traffic jams often result from the incredible number of vehicles on the nation's roads and highways. Traffic jams are especially a problem in large cities, where thousands of cars and trucks crowd the streets. The infrastructure is unable to handle such heavy traffic.

Originally developed around the same time as the country's road system, mass transit systems help ease traffic jams in the cities. Trains, subways, and buses can move **commuters** quickly and efficiently. Commuter trains speed beneath the streets or race along tracks overhead, avoiding the roads altogether.

SPOTLIGHT ON

Suspension Bridges

Countless bridges were built as crucial parts of the highway network. The most dramatic of these are suspension bridges. The main span of a suspension bridge is supported by a graceful arch of cables. The longest suspension bridge in the United States is the Verrazano-Narrows Bridge in New York. The country's most photographed suspension bridge is the Golden Gate Bridge (above) in San Francisco.

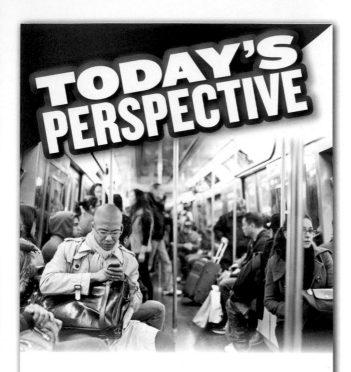

New York City has the most extensive subway system of any city in the United States. The New York subway system has 468 stations and carries about 5.3 million riders each weekday. The system works so well that many New Yorkers never bother learning to drive.

Up in the Air

Today, flying is usually the fastest way for travelers to go from one city to another. Commercial air travel began in 1918, when planes flew mail from city to city. These mail planes occasionally took passengers along on their runs. The passengers had to sit on sacks of letters.

By 1930, 38 airline companies were providing service to passengers within the United States. At that time, a plane could carry about 10 passengers. A cross-country trip took 36 hours, including an overnight stop, usually in Kansas City, Missouri. Transatlantic passenger service began in 1939, with regular flights from New York to London, England.

The jet age truly dawned during the 1950s. Powerful jet engines propelled larger planes that carried as many as 200 passengers. As planes grew bigger and faster, they could carry more and more people on each flight.

Many companies use the airways to carry cargo instead of people. The largest of these cargo carriers is Federal Express, based in Memphis, Tennessee. Because of FedEx, as the carrier is widely known, Memphis International Airport moves more cargo than any other airport in the world. Every day, FedEx speeds packages from Memphis to more than 350 destinations.

The Information Revolution

The wonder of radio came to U.S. households during the 1920s. Each night, families across the country gathered around radios to hear *The Shadow*, *The Lone Ranger*, and other favorite programs. The radio made news and entertainment available with the turn of a knob.

Radios of the 1920s and 1930s were much larger than those commonly used today.

Early televisions displayed black-and-white images on small screens.

In the late 1940s, television began transmitting pictures along with sound. Within a few years, the typical American was spending several hours a day watching TV. Broadcasting stations and the signals that brought radio and television into American homes became a key part of the nation's infrastructure.

As early as the 1960s, computer scientists thought about using the telephone lines to communicate between computers. They hoped that someday vast stores of information could be shared from one computer to another. These connections formed the earliest version of the Internet. Over the following decades, a sprawling network of information and entertainment sites developed. It came to be known as the World Wide Web.

The Internet made it possible for people to send messages from one computer to another. E-mail began to replace old-fashioned letters. Instead of visiting "brick-and-mortar" stores, millions of people discovered the ease of shopping online. Through vast information networks such as Google, people could find anything from advice on which car to buy to the complete works of famous authors. They could listen to their favorite music or hear the sounds of a humpback whale.

Radio, television, and the Internet have brought people together as never before in history. Distances seem to shrink as messages fly across thousands of miles at the speed of thought.

When the Infrastructure Breaks Down

On October 31, 2012, Superstorm Sandy struck the East Coast of the United States. High winds lashed New York, New Jersey, Connecticut, and a half dozen other states. Pouring rain overwhelmed sewer systems and flooded roads. Falling trees ripped down power lines, and millions of households lost electricity. Telephone and Internet service came to a halt.

The infrastructure is designed to function under extreme conditions, but the existing systems could not withstand Sandy's assault. People from West Virginia to

Superstorm Sandy caused as many as 10 million households and businesses to lose power.

Maine lost power. In some places, power was not restored for two weeks or more. It was as though the storm victims were thrown some 200 years backward in time.

People centuries ago were equipped to live without electricity and high-speed transportation. Today, we depend on the infrastructure for everything from food to emergency help. Many people no longer have fireplaces to heat their homes. They do not grow their own food as our ancestors did. Most do not have horses to ride when they have to go for help. Our cars will not run unless we can fill their tanks with gasoline.

Events such as Superstorm Sandy reveal serious weaknesses in our infrastructure. Yet natural disasters are not the only concerns that plague the nation's leaders. The infrastructure's dependence on computers places it in danger of **cyberterrorism**. Cyberterrorist attacks could interfere with the operation of business, banking, and the government.

Another serious concern about the infrastructure is maintenance. It costs money to maintain highways, railroads, and bridges. Without proper care, roads may wear away and bridges may weaken or even collapse. It is not enough merely to build a strong infrastructure. The existing infrastructure requires constant care and attention.

Regular maintenance keeps highways smooth and strong.

MAP OF THE EVENTS
What Happened Where?

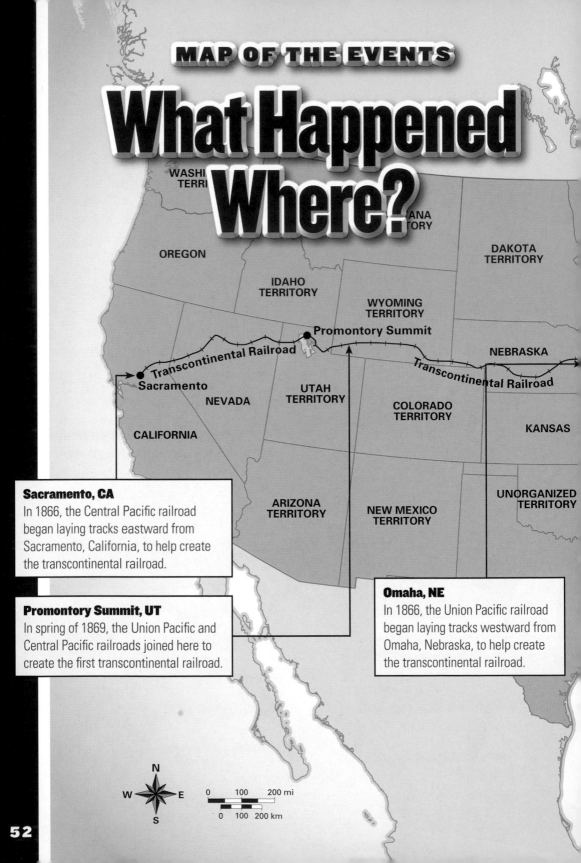

WASHI
TERRI

OREGON

ANA
TORY

DAKOTA
TERRITORY

IDAHO
TERRITORY

WYOMING
TERRITORY

Promontory Summit

Transcontinental Railroad

NEBRASKA

Transcontinental Railroad

Sacramento

NEVADA

UTAH
TERRITORY

COLORADO
TERRITORY

KANSAS

CALIFORNIA

Sacramento, CA
In 1866, the Central Pacific railroad began laying tracks eastward from Sacramento, California, to help create the transcontinental railroad.

ARIZONA
TERRITORY

NEW MEXICO
TERRITORY

UNORGANIZED
TERRITORY

Promontory Summit, UT
In spring of 1869, the Union Pacific and Central Pacific railroads joined here to create the first transcontinental railroad.

Omaha, NE
In 1866, the Union Pacific railroad began laying tracks westward from Omaha, Nebraska, to help create the transcontinental railroad.

N
W E
S

0 100 200 mi

0 100 200 km

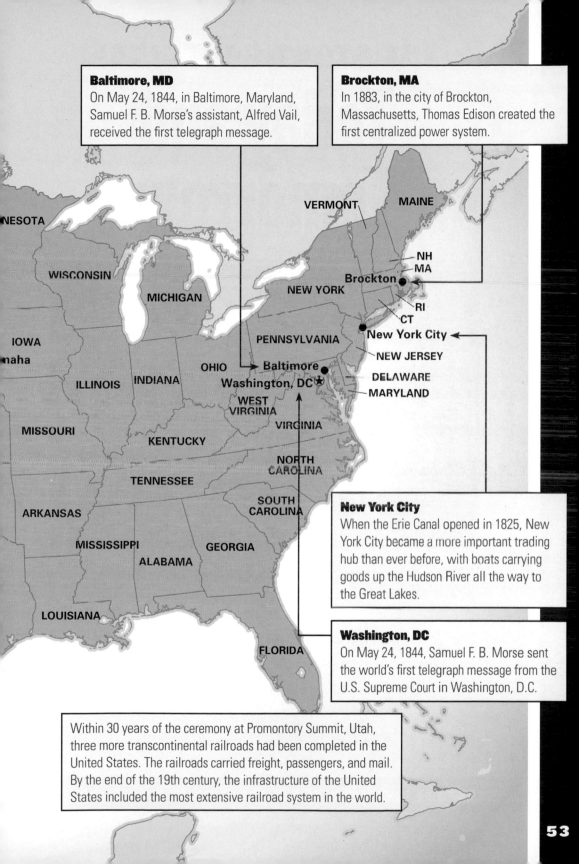

Baltimore, MD
On May 24, 1844, in Baltimore, Maryland, Samuel F. B. Morse's assistant, Alfred Vail, received the first telegraph message.

Brockton, MA
In 1883, in the city of Brockton, Massachusetts, Thomas Edison created the first centralized power system.

New York City
When the Erie Canal opened in 1825, New York City became a more important trading hub than ever before, with boats carrying goods up the Hudson River all the way to the Great Lakes.

Washington, DC
On May 24, 1844, Samuel F. B. Morse sent the world's first telegraph message from the U.S. Supreme Court in Washington, D.C.

Within 30 years of the ceremony at Promontory Summit, Utah, three more transcontinental railroads had been completed in the United States. The railroads carried freight, passengers, and mail. By the end of the 19th century, the infrastructure of the United States included the most extensive railroad system in the world.

Today and Tomorrow

Wireless Internet networks are just one part of modern infrastructure.

The development of the infrastructure has transformed life for people in the United States. Additionally, the systems of a global infrastructure now link people all over the world. You can use a computer to talk to a friend in Saudi Arabia or read the headlines in an Australian newspaper. You can

SOUTH KOREA HAS FASTER INTERNET

watch a video of your cousin's birthday party or follow a scientific expedition to the Pacific Ocean floor.

Day by day and hour by hour, creative minds all over the world are planning the infrastructure of tomorrow. Perhaps they will find safer and more efficient sources of energy. Perhaps they will develop translation programs that will melt away the world's language barriers and allow the people of all nations to communicate with ease. Maybe they will develop a form of transportation that will free our cities from traffic jams forever.

Two hundred years ago, no one could have imagined the infrastructure that we enjoy today. We can only wonder and marvel at the possibilities for the infrastructure of the future.

People in the United States spend a combined 14.5 million hours per day in traffic jams.

CONNECTIONS THAN ANY OTHER COUNTRY.

INFLUENTIAL INDIVIDUALS

Robert Fulton

Robert Fulton (1765–1815) was an engineer and inventor who developed the first commercially successful steamboat.

Henry Shreve (1785–1851) was a shipbuilder who designed vessels for the shallow waters of the Mississippi River.

Samuel F. B. Morse (1791–1872) is credited with the invention of the telegraph. He was the first inventor to make the telegraph commercially successful.

Peter Cooper (1791–1883) was an engineer who built the locomotive *Tom Thumb*.

Alexander Graham Bell (1847–1922) invented the first commercially successful telephone.

Thomas Edison (1847–1931) was the inventor of the incandescent lightbulb and the first electrical power station. Among his many other inventions were the first voting machine, the phonograph, and the motion picture.

Peter Cooper

Thomas Edison

TIMELINE

1788
John Fitch opens a steamboat service on the Delaware River between Philadelphia, Pennsylvania, and Burlington, New Jersey.

1807
Robert Fulton's steamboat, the *Clermont*, carries passengers up the Hudson River from New York City to Albany, New York.

1811
Construction begins on the National Road, which eventually stretches from Cumberland, Maryland, to Vandalia, Illinois.

1830
A horse-drawn train wins a race against the locomotive *Tom Thumb*.

1844
Samuel F. B. Morse sends the first telegraph message from Washington, D.C., to Baltimore, Maryland.

1877
Alexander Graham Bell and Thomas Watson have the world's first telephone conversation.

1879
Thomas Edison invents the incandescent lightbulb.

1913
The Lincoln Highway opens as the nation's first transcontinental highway.

1825

The Erie Canal is completed, connecting the Hudson River with Lake Erie.

1826

The Granite Railway carries stone to Boston Harbor from a quarry in Quincy, Massachusetts.

1858

The transatlantic cable is laid between the United States and Great Britain.

1861

Western Union completes the first transcontinental telegraph line.

1869

The Union Pacific and Central Pacific railroads meet at Promontory Summit, Utah, completing the first transcontinental railroad line.

1939

Transatlantic air service begins from New York to London.

1991

The World Wide Web becomes available to the public.

LIVING HISTORY

Primary sources provide firsthand evidence about a topic. Witnesses to a historical event create primary sources. They include autobiographies, newspaper reports of the time, oral histories, photographs, and memoirs. A secondary source analyzes primary sources and is one step or more removed from the event. Secondary sources include textbooks, encyclopedias, and commentaries. To view the following primary and secondary sources, go to www.factsfornow.scholastic.com. Enter the keywords **U.S. Infrastructure** and look for the Living History logo Σ¡.

Σ¡ **The Erie Canal Museum** The Erie Canal Museum, located in Syracuse, New York, is housed in the Weighlock Building, which dates back to 1850. It has been preserved over time as a valuable reminder of what travel was like more than a hundred years ago in the United States.

Σ¡ **The Lincoln Highway** The Lincoln Highway was the first road to stretch all the way across the United States from the Atlantic coast to the Pacific coast. Today, people often drive across the entire length of the road in order to experience a historic route in American travel.

Σ¡ **The Museum of Communications** Located in Seattle, Washington, the Museum of Communications preserves antique telephone equipment in order to provide visitors with a glimpse into the history of telecommunications. Much of the museum's technology is in working condition.

Σ¡ **The National Railroad Museum** The National Railroad Museum opened in 1958 in Green Bay, Wisconsin, to preserve the history of U.S. railroads by displaying antique train cars and other important artifacts. Visitors can step aboard restored train cars to see firsthand what it was like to travel by rail decades ago.

RESOURCES

Books

Kendall, Martha E. *The Erie Canal*. Washington, DC: National Geographic, 2008.

McCormick, Anita Louise. *The Invention of the Telegraph and Telephone in American History*. Berkeley Heights, NJ: Enslow Publishing, 2004.

Perritano, John. *The Transcontinental Railroad*. New York: Children's Press, 2010.

Worth, Richard. *Telegraph and Telephone*. Milwaukee, WI: World Almanac Library, 2006.

Visit this Scholastic Web site for more information on U.S. infrastructure:
www.factsfornow.scholastic.com
Enter the keywords U.S. Infrastructure

GLOSSARY

commuters (kuh-MYOO-turz) people who travel some distance to work or school each day, usually by car, bus, or train

cyberterrorism (SYE-bur-ter-ur-iz-uhm) a form of terrorism that targets computers and networks over the Internet

economy (i-KAHN-uh-mee) the system of buying, selling, making things, and managing money in a place

engineer (en-juh-NEER) someone who is specially trained to design and build machines or large structures such as bridges and roads

industry (IN-duh-stree) a single branch of business or trade

infrastructure (IN-fruh-struk-chur) the underlying systems that allow something to function

locomotives (loh-kuh-MOH-tivs) engines used to push or pull railroad cars

sanitation (san-uh-TAY-shuhn) systems for cleaning the water supply and disposing of sewage and garbage in a town or city

towpaths (TOH-paths) narrow roads along the banks of a canal, traveled by mules as they hauled canal boats

transcontinental (trans-kahn-tuh-NEN-tuhl) spanning the entire distance of a continent

INDEX

Page numbers in *italics* indicate illustrations.

air travel, 46–47
Allen, Horatio, 21–22, *21*
American Civil War, 28, *28*

Baltimore and Ohio Railroad, *18*, 19
Bell, Alexander Graham, 35, 36, 37, *37*, 57
bridges, 22, 28, *43*, 45, *45*, 51
Buchanan, James, 33–34

canals, 12–14, *13*, *14*, 15, *21*
cargo. *See* freight.
Carroll, Charles, 19
Central Pacific Railroad, 28–29
Chicago, Illinois, 25–26, *25*
Clermont steamboat, 15
colonists, *8*, *9*, 10
computers, 48–49, 51, 54
Cooper, Peter, 22, *23*, 57, *57*
Cumberland Road. *See* National Road.
cyberterrorism, 51

Dickens, Charles, 24

Edison, Thomas, 39, *39*, 57, *57*
Eisenhower, Dwight D., 43–45
electricity, 6–7, *6*, 31, 33, 39, 41, 49, 50, *50*, 57
e-mail, 49
Erie Canal, 12–13, *13*, *14*

Federal Express (FedEx), 47
Fitch, John, 15
freight, 16, 17, *18*, 23, 47
Fulton, Robert, 15, *15*, 56, *56*

Golden Gate Bridge, 45, *45*
gold rush, 27, *27*
Great Britain, 10, 14, 15, 21, 34

Hawthorne, Nathaniel, 24
highways, 7, 43–45, *43*, *44*, 51, *51*. *See also* roadways.
horses, 9, 10, 20–21, *20*, 22, *30*, 31, 50

industry, 14, 37, 38, 51
Internet, 48–49, 54–55, *54*

jet engines, 46

lightbulbs, 39, 57
Lincoln Highway, 43, *43*, 44
locomotives, 21–23, *22*, 24, 29, 57
Louisiana Territory, 26
Lyons-Fulton Bridge, *43*

mail, *30*, 31, 46, 49
maintenance, 51, *51*
map, *52–53*
mass transit systems, 45, 46, *46*
Memphis International Airport, 47
Mexican-American War, 26, *26*
mining, 14, 20, 27, *27*
Mississippi River, 16, 17, 28, *43*, 56
Morse, Samuel F. B., 32–33, *32*, 56
Museum of Communications, 36

National Railroad Museum, 29
National Road, 10–12, *11*
natural gas, 38, *38*
New Orleans steamboat, 16

population, 25, 27, 41

radio, 47, *47*, 48, 49
railroads, *18*, 19, 20–23, *20*, *22*,
  24–26, *25*, 27–29, *29*, 41, 51, 57
roadways, 7, 10–12, *10*, *11*, 14,
  21, 41, 44, 49, *55*. *See also*
  highways.

Savery, Thomas, 14
settlers, *8*, 9, 10–12, *10*, 25, 26
sewage systems, 7, 38, 49
Shreve, Henry, 16, 56
South Korea, 54–55
steamboats, 15–17, *16*, 56
steam engines, 14, 21, 24
Stourbridge Lion locomotive,
  21–22, *22*, 23
subway systems, 45, 46, *46*
Superstorm Sandy, 49–50, *50*, 51
switchboards, 36, *36*

telegraph, 32–34, *32*, *33*, *34*, 41, 56
telephones, 6, 7, 35–37, *36*, *40*,
  41, 48, 49, 57

television, 48, *48*, 49
Tom Thumb locomotive, 22–23,
  57
towpaths, 14
traffic jams, 45, 55, *55*
transatlantic cable, 35
transcontinental railroad, 28–29,
  29
transcontinental telegraph line,
  34, *34*
Twain, Mark, 17, *17*

Union Pacific Railroad, 28–29

Vail, Alfred, 32
Verrazano-Narrows Bridge, 45
Victoria, queen of Great Britain, 34

water, 6–7, 38, 41, *42*
Watson, Thomas, 35, 37
Weighlock Building, 12
Western Union company, 34
World Wide Web, 49

ABOUT THE AUTHOR

Deborah Kent grew up in Little Falls, New Jersey, where she was the first totally blind student to attend public school. She graduated from Oberlin College and earned a master's degree from Smith College School for Social Work. She worked in community mental health at New York's University Settlement House before she moved to the Mexican town of San Miguel de Allende to devote herself to writing. She is the author of nearly two dozen young-adult novels and numerous nonfiction titles for young readers, including several books in the Cornerstones of Freedom series. She lives in Chicago with her husband, children's author R. Conrad Stein.